W9-APC-789

Hispanic Heritage

Hispanic Heritage

Title List

Latino Americans and Immigration Laws

Crossing the Border

by Miranda Hunter

Mason Crest Publishers

Philadelphia

Mason Crest Publishers Inc.

370 Reed Road, Broomall, Pennsylvania 19008

(866) MCP-BOOK (toll free)

www.masoncrest.com

First edition, 2005

13 12 11 10 09 08 07 06   10 9 8 7 6 5 4 3 2

Library of Congress Cataloging-in-Publication Data

Hunter, Miranda, 1977–
   Latino Americans and immigration laws : crossing the border / by Miranda Hunter.
      p. cm. — (Hispanic heritage (Philadelphia, Pa.))
   Includes index.
   ISBN 1-59084-939-6   ISBN 1-59084-924-8 (series)
   1. Emigration and immigration law—United States—Juvenile literature. 2. Hispanic Americans—Legal status, laws, etc.—United States—Juvenile literature.   I. Title. II. Hispanic heritage (Philadelphia, Pa.)
   KF4819.6.H86 2005
   342.7308'2—dc22

                              2004020830

Interior design by Dianne Hodack.

Produced by Harding House Publishing Service, Inc., Vestal, NY.

www.hardinghousepages.com

Cover design by Dianne Hodack.

Printed in the Hashemite Kingdom of Jordan.

Contents

Welcoming Our Newest Citizens!

THE 11TH ANNUAL NATURALIZATION
AND SWEARING-IN CEREMONY

....

SEATTLE

.... 11:00 AM - 12:00 NOON

BLUE ANGEL S...

SEATTLE NAV...

Introduction

by José E. Limón, Ph.D.

Even before there was a United States, Hispanics were present in what would become this country. Beginning in the sixteenth century, Spanish explorers traversed North America, and their explorations encouraged settlement as early as the sixteenth century in what is now northern New Mexico and Florida, and as late as the mid-eighteenth century in what is now southern Texas and California.

Later, in the nineteenth century, following Spain's gradual withdrawal from the New World, Mexico in particular established its own distinctive presence in what is now the southwestern part of the United States, a presence reinforced in the first half of the twentieth century by substantial immigration from that country. At the close of the nineteenth century, the U.S. war with Spain brought Cuba and Puerto Rico into an interactive relationship with the United States, the latter in a special political and economic affiliation with the United States even as American power influenced the course of almost every other Latin American country.

The books in this series remind us of these historical origins, even as each explores the present reality of different Hispanic groups. Some of these books explore the contemporary social origins—what social scientists call the "push" factors—behind the accelerating Hispanic immigration to America: political instability, economic underdevelopment and crisis, environmental degradation, impoverished or wholly absent educational systems, and other circumstances contribute to many Latin Americans deciding they will be better off in the United States.

And, for the most part, they will be. The vast majority come to work and work very hard, in order to earn better wages than they would back home. They fill significant labor needs in the U.S. economy and contribute to the economy through lower consumer prices and sales taxes.

When they leave their home countries, many immigrants may initially fear that they are leaving behind vital and important aspects of their home cultures: the Spanish language, kinship ties, food, music, folklore, and the arts. But as these books also make clear, culture is a fluid thing, and these native cultures are not only brought to America, they are also replenished in the United States in fascinating and novel ways. These books further suggest to us that Hispanic groups enhance American culture as a whole.

Our country—especially the young, future leaders who will read these books—can only benefit by the fair and full knowledge these authors provide about the socio-historical origins and contemporary cultural manifestations of America's Hispanic heritage.

Bearer's photograph pasted here

...ht hand

1

The Roads to El Norte

A babble of voices filled the room, some speaking Spanish and some speaking English. Concha felt tired but satisfied. Most of the people she cared about in the world were here today to celebrate her birthday. As she closed her eyes and thought back over her long life, full of joys and sorrow, she felt a little hand pulling on her skirt. She opened her eyes to see her great-granddaughter Carmen smiling up at her. "*Abuela*, are you sleeping? We want you to tell us a story."

This young Latin girl has a long and rich heritage.

Concha looked thoughtfully at Carmen and the other kids, great-grandchildren, grandchildren, great-nieces, and nephews. After a moment, she said, "I'll tell you what my abuela used to tell me when I was little like you all.

"We used to sit at our abuela's knee while she told us about El Norte, about America. We were still in Mexico then, but my uncle was already here. Abuela had never been here, but she had heard many stories. She told us of a place where everyone who wanted a job could have one, where there was always enough food to eat, where *niñas* go to school. We dreamed of someday traveling north to this wonderful land. We begged for stories of El Norte, like you now beg for stories of our homeland.

"Now you have all seen it. Some of you were even born here. What do you think? Do you like El Norte? Do you like the great America?"

Most of the kids nodded, but some of them shook their heads. One of the older children, García, said, "I don't like it here. The teachers at school talk too fast, and I can't understand them. I miss my big brother who is still in Mexico."

Carmen smiled and said, "I love it here! I've never even been to Mexico. This is my home!"

IN TESTIMONY whereof, and by virtue of the authority in me vested by Act No. 46 of the Legislature of Porto Rico, U. S. A., approved April 28, 1930, this

CERTIFICATE OF IDENTIFICATION

is issued at New York City, N. Y., this 21st day of February , 1931.

M. P. Saldaña

M. T. SALDAÑA

Acting Head, New York Branch,
Bureau of Commerce and Industry.

Certificate of Identification for a Puerto Rican immigrant

The "Golden Door"

El Norte, Spanish for "the North," a term for the United States used by our Spanish-speaking neighbors, is a popular destination for many Latinos around the world. Some come here just to work, and others come to make permanent homes. Although the United States is a country made up almost entirely of immigrants, modern America has a vast system of complicated laws and government bodies responsible for controlling who can and cannot be part of today's "American Dream."

People all over the world seek to enter the United States for a variety of reasons. Those reasons can be broken down into two categories. The first category is called *push factors*, circumstances that push people to leave their home countries. These reasons are problems at home including underdevelopment, poverty, government corruption, low wages, lack of jobs, political strife, and overpopulation. The second category is *pull factors*, conditions in the United States that pull people here. These factors

Melting Pot—or Mosaic?

ave you ever seen a mosaic? A mosaic is a beautiful image made of many unique pieces of broken glass or pottery, or even torn pieces of paper, joined together to create a new picture. Each small piece was once part of some other "whole." Now, each piece joins other pieces—some like it, some completely different—to make something new.

Historically, the United States was called a melting pot. Immigrants who came to this country were expected to give up the traditions, "the ways," of their homeland to become an American. The newcomers would adopt the mainstream culture, and all would become one. There would be no way to tell the immigrant from the native-born—all would become one, perhaps the same?

The idea of the United States as a melting pot is not a popular one with many groups today. They don't like the idea of being told that they must destroy their heritage to become an American. To them, and many native-born citizens as well, the concept of America as a mosaic is much more appealing. Each person retains the characteristics of their heritage, jagged edges and all, and joins with other people who retain their heritage, and together, something bigger and more beautiful is made. The individual remains an individual, and the country benefits from what each individual brings to the picture.

include higher wages, jobs, higher standard of living, and freedom from violence. These factors have a greater effect on people who are poor in their home countries because they have far less to lose by leaving.

The United States is a country that was built into what it is today by immigration. Very few U.S. citizens can trace their ancestry back to the Native American people who lived here before the arrival of European settlers. The country has been proudly called the "great melting pot," but this is really a reference to the past rather than the future. For various reasons, most Americans no longer like to use this term.

Ellis Island, the home of the Statue of Liberty, is the gateway through which more than 12 million immigrants passed into the United States seeking their chance to make their lives better. The statue herself was designed as a symbol of the opportunity represented by the United States. Lady Liberty stands in New York Harbor, holding up her light to guide the way for immigrants of centuries past. At her feet stands a plaque engraved with a poem called "The New Colossus" by Emma Lazarus. In this poem, Lady Liberty speaks,

Give me your tired, your poor,
Your huddled masses yearning to breathe free,
The wretched refuse of your teeming shore.
Send these, the homeless, tempest-tost to me,
I lift my lamp beside the golden door!

liberal: tolerant of different views, standards of behavior, and not opposed to change.

conservative: cautious; reluctant to accept change.

restrictive: acting as a limit to control something.

Although this poem extends an invitation to the poor and desperate, today's immigration law is far less welcoming to many people in need throughout the world.

U.S. Immigration Policy

.S. immigration policy must be viewed in the context of two opposing tensions, one pulling for a more *liberal*, welcoming policy and the other straining toward a more *conservative, restrictive* policy.

A variety of factors influence the urge toward a more liberal policy. Travel and communication have become very easy in recent years, and the world is interconnected and interdependent. Many foreign companies now operate in the United States, and increasing numbers of U.S. companies operate in foreign countries. As a result, the international business community expects to be able to transfer its workforce where it needs, regardless of the political boundaries of countries. In addition, many Americans see the United States as having a unique position in the world—protector and helpmate to nations and people from all over the globe. America has the resources and, some would say, the responsibility to share the wealth and freedom that it has fostered within its borders.

Other factors lead the United States toward a less welcoming, more conservative immigration policy. The U.S. population has grown significantly throughout its history, and some believe that further growth would be bad for the country. Many of the people who seek to enter the United States come from very different cultural backgrounds. Some Americans fear diver-

In a mosaic each small piece contributes to the total design.

sity and even see these differences as a threat to the "American" way of life. The perception that immigrants take jobs from citizens and act as a drain on society by committing crimes and collecting welfare leads to pressure to keep as many "foreigners" as possible out of the country. Since noncitizens cannot vote, politicians can blame immigrants for a variety of social problems without having to worry about losing their political support. In addition, concerns about national security, especially in the days since September 11, 2001, have increased concerns about noncitizens entering the country.

Over the years, immigrants have usually come to America in waves from specific countries as conditions in those countries pushed people out. Drought, famine, religious persecution, war, and other unfavorable circumstances have led people to seek safety in the United States. Although this continues to be true, more and more people in more recent years have come to America temporarily to accomplish specific goals, such as learning the language, getting a college degree, or earning enough money to make themselves or their families comfortable in their home country.

The U.S. government has taken on the responsibility of creating a system to regulate and control who enters the country and under what circumstances. At its most basic, U.S. immigration law says that noncitizens who enter this country must have a visa, or a stamp, placed on their passports (the paperwork that each country provides its citizens to prove who they are and where they are from), which legally allows entrance into the United States. A complicated system of laws decides who can get these visas and who cannot.

Visas fall into two categories: immigrant and nonimmigrant. Immigrant visas are issued to people to allow them to make their homes permanently in the United States. Nonimmigrant, or temporary, visas allow foreign individuals to come into the country for a specific purpose or a stated period of time. As most people are aware, however, millions of people have entered and continue to enter the United States without the proper paperwork. These people live and work in the country, some for short periods and others for a lifetime.

Latinos are now the fastest growing ethnic group in the United States. Some have come to the country very recently, while others have been here as long as any Europeans. Although some have entered the country illegally, millions have come here within the bounds of the law. They are a vital part of American culture and economy—and they are here to stay.

Migrate, Emigrate, Immigrate; Migrant, Emigrant, Immigrant

he terminology used can sometimes be confusing. These six words sound similar and are all related, but each means something different. If a person *migrates*, he moves from one place to another and can be called a *migrant*. If he *emigrates*, he leaves his home country. That person would be an *emigrant*. If he moves into another country with the intention of staying, that means that he *immigrates*, and he could be called an *immigrant*.

Habla Español

gente (hane-tay): people

niñas (neen-yahs): little girls

abuela (ah-bway-lah): grandmother

dinero (dee-nare-oh): money

trabajo (trah-bah-hoe): work

2

History of Immigration Law and Policy

Carmen, always the boldest of the *niños*, said, "Abuela, please tell us another story. Tell us how you came to America!"

Concha smiled down at her, "I've told you this one a hundred times. You don't really want to hear it again, do you?"

Carmen and the other children nodded. So Concha began, "This was more than eighty years ago now. I was just a girl of fifteen, just a few months after my birthday, my *quinceaño*. Our country had been at war with itself for as long as I could remember, but this year was especially bad. We had a new president who shut down all the Catholic schools, including the one where my brothers went. There was fighting all around us. My parents were getting more and more scared. They decided it was time to join my Uncle José in Texas, where my father could work on a ranch with him. Tío José had applied for papers for us to cross the border, and for ages we had been saving any money that we could get because we had to pay fifty American cents for each one of us to go across. That may not sound like a lot of money to you, but that was a vast sum to us. We were lucky, too, because Mamá and Papá could both read and write. My grandparents could not get visas because they could not read.

"We took a train north. It was hot and crowded on the train, but we did not mind because we were on our way to America. It took us days and days, but eventually we reached the border. After Mamá and Papá showed the papers to the men at the border, they let us go across. We were so surprised that America did not look any different than Mexico. It was hot and dusty, but Tío José was waiting for us. We all hugged and kissed and cried. We were in America!"

Nineteenth-Century Immigration Regulation

he United States was not always concerned about controlling immigration. In the early days of the country, the borders were relatively free and easy to cross: no visas, no green cards, no Border Patrol. Port cities teemed with life as immigrants stepped off the boats with the "American Dream" in their hearts. The country had plenty of room for everyone. In fact, the country had no formal policy about immigration until after the end of the U.S. Civil War. At that point, some states began passing laws regulating immigration. In response, the U.S. Supreme Court in 1875 declared immigration regulation a federal responsibility, starting a cascade of immigration laws that led to today's complex system of regulations.

As the number of immigrants continued to rise, economic conditions began to worsen, and some parts of the country began to experience overcrowding. Congress took notice and passed the very first immigration law, known as the Immigration Act of 1882, which called for a tax of fifty cents per head and blocked the entry of "idiots, lunatics, convicts, and persons likely to become a *public charge*." In addition to this law, the Chinese Exclusion Act of 1882 was passed. This blocked the immigration of Chinese people into the country.

public charge: someone likely to become dependent on government social services for support.

The addition of the Alien Contract Labor laws of 1885 and 1887, which limited the immigration of certain types of workers, forced the government to set up an agency to deal with enforcement of the new regulations. At that point, the states were responsible for enforcing immigration laws under the guidance of the U.S. Treasury Department. U.S. Customs officials at each port collected the head tax, and "Chinese Inspectors" made sure that no Chinese immigrants came into the country. The passage of the Immigration Act of 1891 added more rules about who could come into the country, making enforcement more difficult. It included the creation of a new Office of the Superintendent of Immigration within the Treasury Department. The superintendent oversaw the activities of newly hired immigration inspectors placed in the major port cities around the country.

The 1891 law required that the federal government assume the responsibility of inspecting and processing all immigrants.

APPLICATION FOR A CERTIFICATE OF IDENTIFICATION

(FORM FOR MALE APPLICANTS)

#1525

UNITED STATES OF AMERICA,

The People of Porto Rico } ss:

City of New York

I, _Bernardo Vega_, a Native of Porto Rico and a loyal citizen of the United States of America, hereby apply to the Head of the New York Branch, Bureau of Commerce and Industry of Porto Rico, for a certificate of identification as a citizen of the United States born in Porto Rico.

I solemnly swear that I was born at _Cayey,_ in the Island of Porto Rico, on or about _January 14, 1885_; that my {father} _Antonio Vega_, was born in _Patillas, P. R._, and is now residing at _Deceased_; that I am domiciled in the United States, my permanent residence being at _786 Eta Belmont Ave, Elmont N.Y._; that I became a citizen of the United States by (1) _Act of Congress of March 2, 1917_

(2) _____

In case of an accident, _Mrs. Lena Vega_ whose address is _786 Belmont Ave., Elmont N.Y._, should be notified.

Bernardo Vega
[Applicant's Signature]

Sworn to before me this _2nd_ day of _November_, 193_6_.

M. T. Dardain

Head of the New York Branch, Bureau of Commerce and Industry.

(1) Act of Congress of March 2, 1917. (Organic Act of Porto Rico.)
(2) By naturalization.

This form was part of the paperwork required for immigration.

22

As part of that responsibility, they began to make an effort to collect and check the passenger lists (called manifests) from each ship that came into port. Many experts think of this as the first real national immigration policy.

The Advent of the Twentieth Century

From 1895 to 1903, Congress modified the Office of the Superintendent of Immigration to make it a federal bureau and moved it into the newly created Department of Commerce and Labor. The new bureau's responsibilities were expanded to include enforcement of all laws regarding immigration, removing that burden from the states.

Congress soon began working on the issue of naturalization, a method for people not born in the country to become citizens. The U.S. Constitution gives the responsibility for naturalization to Congress, but the huge caseload of applicants for citizenship was far too large for Congress to handle. Therefore, in 1902, Congress authorized any court of law in the United States to review and accept naturalization requests. Congress continued its oversight of the process, finding that the five thousand courts that handled naturalization were not very consistent.

In an effort to standardize naturalization, Congress passed the Basic Naturalization Act of 1906. The rules laid out in that act are still used as the basis of naturalization law today. It established the use of standard forms for naturalization nationwide and expanded the Bureau of Immigration into the Bureau of Immigration and Naturalization. State and local courts were also encouraged to give up their naturalization duties to federal courts in an effort to control the interpretation of the regulations. The naturalization service began checking records of all naturalization hearings nationwide.

literate: able to read and write.

In response to a massive upswing of immigration in the first years of the twentieth century, Congress made immigration laws even more restrictive with the Immigration Act of 1907. This law increased the head tax and placed more limits on immigrants, including keeping out all Japanese immigrants, orphans, and people with physical or mental defects.

World War I

residential and congressional committees were established to study the reasons for the surge in immigration and the living conditions of those already in this country. The findings of these commissions are reflected in the Immigration Act of 1917, which, among other things, excluded those who could not read and write at least one language. The increased immigration also caused the formation of the U.S. Immigration Service to deal with the influx of people, which began testing immigrants to make certain that only those who were *literate* were allowed into the country. This law (and the U.S. entrance into World War I) greatly reduced immigration for several years. This was the first act of Congress that had a major impact on Latino immigration, because many could not read and write well enough to pass the exams.

During World War I, a presidential proclamation by Woodrow Wilson required the use of passports for all U.S. citi-

U. S. CUSTOMS S

PORT OF NEW YO

Pass *Jesús Colón*

Address *147 W. 143*

Nationality *Porto Ri*

Occupation *Salesman*

Employed by *Nationa*

Pass issued on request *of E la*

Acting for said *Corpora*

281049

A customs' card

zens, which caused great delays all along the U.S.-Mexico and U.S.-Canada borders. The Immigration Service began issuing border-crossing cards for those interested in crossing the borders for a short time, greatly increasing paperwork for the Immigration Service.

Illegal Immigration

t the end of World War I, mass immigration resumed. Congress responded with the Immigration Act of 1924, which established a system for limiting the number of immigrants accepted from each country. Only immigrants holding a valid visa could enter the United States, and each nation was assigned a limited number of visas depending on how many immigrants from that country had already entered

repatriation: *the sending back of someone to his or her country of origin, or to the country of which they are a citizen.*

executive order: *a rule issued by the executive branch of government that has the status of a law.*

detention camps: *places where people are detained, often for immigration violations or political reasons.*

America. This new system was called the National Origins Quota System.

The new restrictions caused a major problem for the country: illegal immigration. Until then, the only illegal immigrants were those who were stopped based on the exclusions established by previous laws, such as Chinese or Japanese immigrants. Thousands of those who would have been admitted before 1924 were now being rejected. Congress created the U.S. Border Patrol to control the borders in 1924 because of this new influx of illegal immigrants. This new policy had immediate and obvious effects on Latinos. The Border Patrol was responsible for the long-uncontrolled border between Mexico and the United States that was too easily crossed.

In 1933, existing agencies merged into the Immigration and Naturalization Service (INS). The employees were required to take Civil Service exams to ensure that they met certain standards, which improved the overall performance of the INS. During the 1930s, immigration volume dropped significantly. This was mostly due to the Great Depression, but some government programs had an effect as well. Perhaps the most important of these was a *repatriation* program established between the United States and Mexico that returned Mexican-born individuals to Mexico, some against their will.

As the 1940s began, the threat of war in Europe led to concerns that immigration was a risk to national security. In 1940, President Franklin Delano Roosevelt issued an *executive order* that moved the INS from the Department of Labor to the Department of Justice. Many INS employees volunteered for the war effort after the United States entered the war, leaving the department short of experienced workers and leading to changes in its operations during the war. The INS was asked to record and fingerprint every alien in the country and to organize and maintain *detention camps*. Border Patrol efforts were stepped up to protect the nation from threats.

In spite of security concerns, the lack of American workers caused by many citizens going off to war led to policies that were more liberal in some ways and more restrictive in others. The Bracero Program brought thousands of Mexican workers into the United States as temporary workers to replace the Americans who had gone to war. However, these workers were not authorized to stay in the country, and many were mistreated and paid extremely low wages.

The Cold War

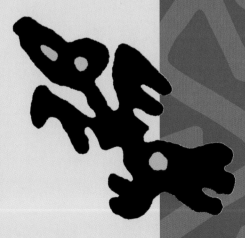

n the years after World War II, several congressional acts affected INS policies. Most important, Congress combined all previous immigration and naturalization laws into the Immigration and Nationality Act of 1952. In addition, the Displaced Persons Act of 1948 and the Refugee Relief Act of 1953 established the guidelines for allowing people affected by the war to enter the United States. The Cold War, with its hostility between the *democratic* portions of the world and the *communist bloc*, affected immigration policy as well. For example, the Cuban Adjustment Program of 1960 allowed individuals from Communist Cuba to enter the United States.

In the mid-1950s, the INS focused its enforcement on two main areas of concern. The public had begun to pressure the government over the presence of illegal immigrants living and working in the United States, so the INS increased efforts to patrol the borders and to *deport* identified illegal immigrants.

democratic: a form of government characterized by equal participation in the decision-making process.

communist bloc: a group of countries that supports communist rule, the system of government in which a single party holds power, and the state controls the economy.

deport: to force a foreigner to leave a country.

This directly affected many Latinos, as they had been able to immigrate over the relatively open and long border between Mexico and the United States easily. The Border Patrol began devising new methods for controlling the border.

The 1960s Through the End of the Twentieth Century

n 1965, Congress *amended* the 1952 act, replacing the National Origins Quota System with a preference system based on family connections or work skills. This system is still in place. The new system continued to limit the number of immigration visas available each year, but organized applicants into categories designed to reunite split families or to bring skilled workers into the country.

One of the most influential acts of Congress, the Immigration Reform and Control Act of 1986, gave the INS the power to place *sanctions* on employers that hired illegal immigrants. The act was accompanied by a short-term *amnesty* program for illegal immigrants present in the United States who wished to obtain legal status before the law went into effect.

The Immigration Act of 1990 revised the Immigration and Nationality Act, which was the basis for most immigration law. Some of the major changes were very important to Latinos. The law included an increase in the number of annual employment-based nonimmigrant visas from 54,000 to 140,000. Since the majority of temporary workers who enter the United States each year are Latino, this change was important to them. It also

The Migration Department's reception desk

added a few changes to other nonimmigrant visa categories and slightly expanded the total number of visas available.

In 1994, the United States created a program called Operation Gatekeeper, designed to decrease illegal immigration. It involved looking much more carefully at the paperwork of people attempting to enter the country to reduce the number of people getting in with false papers. The law also attempted to increase security along the border. As part of this effort, the United States built a ten- to twelve-foot high security fence along a sixty-foot stretch of the U.S. and Mexican border near San Diego, California. As the Border Patrol gained more technology, their equipment included night-vision equipment and sensors that could tell when someone was walking nearby. Although this law was quite successful in reducing illegal immigration in the targeted regions of the country, most experts agree that it did little to reduce the overall numbers coming into the country. Instead, illegal immigrants were forced to use more dangerous routes—but they continued to pour into the United States.

commissions: committees established to study an issue and recommend actions.

he first U.S. law to impose rules on immigration was the Naturalization Act of 1795, which restricted citizenship to "free white persons" who lived in the United States for five years and gave up their allegiance to their former country.

President Bill Clinton asked several *commissions* to study legal and illegal immigration issues, and the result was the Illegal Immigration Reform and Immigrant Responsibility Act of 1996. It brought more major changes to immigration law. The act was designed to create stronger penalties against illegal immigration, simplify and speed the deportation process by limiting the number of court appeals an individual is entitled to make after being rejected, and restrict access to the country by terrorists. It also sought to prevent immigrants from using certain social systems like welfare.

Post–9/11 America

he attacks that occurred in the United States on September 11, 2001, caused a swell of concern over control of the country's borders. People no longer trust that the systems in place are sufficient to prevent terrorists from entering the country and attacking public buildings. The result of this has been the development of new immigration policies designed to stop the flow of illegal immigrants, while encouraging those already in the country to come forward and be counted. In 2003, the U.S. Immigration and Naturalization Service became part of the Department of Homeland Security and was renamed the United States Citizenship and Immigration Services (USCIS).

But despite all these restrictions, Latinos continue to enter the country.

Police patrol both sides of the Mexican-American border.

Habla Español

tío (tee-oh): uncle

quince (keen-say): fifteen

guerra (gay-rah): war

los Estados Unidos (lohs ace-tah-dohs oo-nee-dohs): the United States

país (pah-ees): country

Who, When,
Where, and Why:
Latino Immigration

García spoke up again and said, "Great-Aunt Concha, was your Tío José the same José that was my great-grandpa?"

Concha nodded. García looked puzzled, "If he lived in Texas, then how did I end up being born in Mexico? Why wasn't my family in America already?"

Concha thought for a minute and responded, "That isn't one of the happier stories that I could tell. Sometimes the American government did things that weren't so nice."

Carmen piped up, "Abuela, I don't understand."

During the Depression, many families lost their homes and were forced to travel around the country looking for work.

"Well, *niños*, you've heard of the Great Depression, I'm sure. It was a very poor time. My father lost his job. There was no rain and no work. People who had once been nice to us started to call us names and to hate us. Tío José had worked at the ranch for many years, and the owner kept him on even when things were rough. But that just made the white folks in the area even angrier. We started to hear about people being sent back to Mexico. Tío Jose didn't want to go, but one day some men from the government came and told him that he and his family had been chosen for the program. His youngest son, Juan, was a citizen because he had been born in America, but the rest of the family would have to go. Juan stayed with us, and everybody else had to board a train for Mexico. That, *mi niño*, is how you came to be born in Mexico."

The First Spanish Settlers

Although most Americans probably believe that the United States was first a British colony, in fact, Spanish settlers were actually the first Europeans to establish a permanent colony in North America. The Spanish successfully colonized St. Augustine in Florida, and during the early days of colonization, Spain controlled much of North America.

Mexico gained its independence from Spain in 1821, seizing control of all of present-day Mexico and the northern region of the Viceroyalty of New Spain, which included California, Texas, and New Mexico. The United States and New Mexico soon began trading goods. The Republic of Mexico tried to regulate

United
States

Cuba

Santo Domingo

Eighteenth-Century
Spanish Territory

As this map indicates, much of the Americas was first colonized by the Spanish.

annexed: took over a
territory to add into
another political entity.

The term Chicano,
a word used to
describe Latinos living
in the Mexican terri-
tory that was annexed
by the United States,
was originated by
some Mexican
Americans who did
not like to use the
longer hyphenated
name given to their
ethnic group. It never
gained complete
acceptance because it
was used historically to
describe people of low
socioeconomic status
in Mexico. Today,
however, more and
more Mexican
Americans use the
word to express their
pride in their unique
identity.

this trade, angering many residents of New Mexico. In the meantime, Mexicans living in California began trading with the United States as well. The trade stimulated the interest of many American settlers. As trade increased with California, the United States began considering ways to acquire the region from Mexico.

Texas

In 1821, an American merchant named Moses Austin received permission from Mexico to move three hundred settlers into Texas. The small settlement quickly ballooned in size to thousands of people, and Mexico was forced to grant Texas independence.

In 1845, the United States *annexed* Texas. This angered the Mexican government and led to the Mexican-American War. The war ended with the Treaty of Guadalupe Hidalgo, which awarded the United States the territory that is the modern-day states of California, Utah, Arizona, New Mexico, Nevada, and parts of Colorado and Wyoming. Nearly 80,000 Mexicans lived in these regions. Most were granted U.S. citizenship.

American citizenship was not necessarily in the best interests of these new citizens. Most did not speak English and were living on land granted to them by the Mexican government. The U.S. government refused to recognize most of these land grants without lengthy and expensive court proceedings, resulting in the loss of land for many of the new citizens. They did not comprehend the court system and spoke English so poorly that they

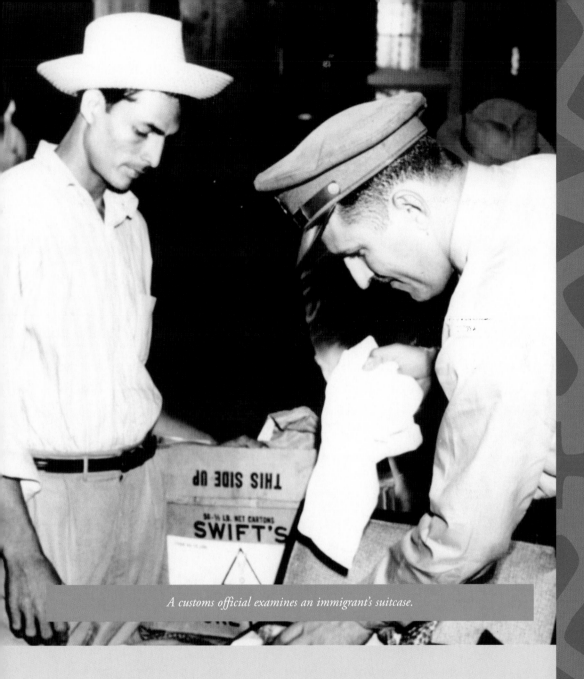

A customs official examines an immigrant's suitcase.

did not understand what was happening to them. Others were forced to sell their land to pay back the loans they took out to pay for the court proceedings.

By the late 1800s, most Mexican Americans were living and working on land that belonged to Anglo-European settlers who had seized their land. They began living together in barrios, which means "neighborhoods" in Spanish and is used to describe Spanish-speaking sections of a town.

Mexican Immigration

Immigration from Mexico and other Latin American countries was extremely low during the late 1800s. Some Mexicans were attracted to farm jobs on ranches in Texas, but overall, immigration was very light. The vast majority of immigrants into the United States came from across the Atlantic Ocean.

In 1900, an estimated 400,000 to 550,000 Mexican Americans were living throughout the country. Economic conditions in Mexico quickly worsened, causing a sharp rise in the number of immigrants to the United States. The Mexican Revolution caused another increase in immigration, as thousands sought to escape the chaos in their home country. This was the beginning of a wave of immigration that eventually saw more than 700,000 Mexicans enter the United States. In the 1920s, about 10 percent of all immigration into the country was from Mexico. Most of the immigrants settled in the Southwest, working at railroads, mines, factories, and farms.

Reading and Writing

In 1917, the United States entered World War I. The economy improved greatly during the war, and Mexican Americans were able to move into better-paying, higher-skilled jobs. However, 1917 was also the year when the United States passed the first truly restrictive immigration law. The law required that all immigrants be able to read and write at least one language, and the Immigration Service gave the tests. Anyone who failed the test could not enter the country. The strict enforcement of this requirement caused a sharp decline in immigration during the 1920s, which lasted until after the Great Depression. Many of the potential immigrants who were turned away were poor Mexicans who would have been accepted prior to the new law.

Sent Back

During the Great Depression, anti-Latino sentiment within the United States grew. Latinos came to be seen as a drain on the economy because they often held less skilled positions, but they were still employed while other Americans were unemployed. When the U.S. and Mexican governments offered a repatriation program, many individuals, like Tío José from our story, were sent back to Mexico against their wishes. Some had families that included children who were born in the United States. These children were, by law, U.S. citizens and were not deported. Some adults who were deported were U.S. citizens as well. In California, detention camps were established where Mexican Americans awaiting deportation were held. The actions angered many and broke up families. Nearly 500,000 Mexican Americans were sent to Mexico by this program.

discrimination: *unfair treatment of a person or group, usually because of prejudice about race, ethnic group, or religion.*

The change in policy also reflected a change in American attitudes toward Latinos. *Discrimination* rose throughout the country. Some restaurants would refuse to serve anyone in a group if a Mexican American was present. Public services were often segregated so that Latinos and European Americans were kept far apart. Schools required children to speak English, and if a student was caught speaking Spanish they were punished, sometimes severely.

The War Years

At the start of World War II, many Latinos volunteered for service. They fought bravely and were awarded more medals per soldier than any other ethnic group. When they returned home, they were unwilling to accept the discrimination they suffered before they left. They formed organizations to fight against the problems they faced. World War II also caused an increased demand for immigrant workers in the United States. There were far more jobs than there were workers, so workers were brought in from Mexico to fill the gaps. High unemployment rates in Mexico meant that these workers took any work they could get, even though they were often mistreated and underpaid by their employers.

Puerto Ricans and Cubans

Immigration of Latinos rose sharply in the years after the war. For the first time, a large number of immigrants from Cuba and Puerto Rico began coming to the United States. Illegal immigration rose as well. New programs designed to stop illegal immigration were developed and instituted, and more than 3.8 million illegal immigrants were deported as a result. The program did little to stop the flow. More illegal immigrants entered than were deported, so no actual gains were being made.

The Puerto Ricans had a special situation. The United States had possessed the rights to the island since 1917, making all Puerto Ricans U.S. citizens. In fact, this means that Puerto Ricans were not immigrants at all, though many Americans treated them as such because they were native Spanish-speakers. However, Puerto Ricans were free to come and go as they pleased. Most came to the mainland United States looking for work, and many settled in the East Harlem section of New York City. Approximately 70 percent of Puerto Ricans living in the United States in 1960 lived in East Harlem. Today, about one-third of all Puerto Ricans living in the United States live in New York City.

Immigration of people from Cuba also presented some unique challenges. Fidel Castro gained power in 1959, and he promptly announced that he was changing the structure of Cuban society. Upper- and middle-class Cubans found his new plan a threat to their way of life, and many left for the United States. In 1962, commercial airlines stopped flying from the United States to Cuba, but this did not stop immigration. The "Boat People," as some Cubans have come to be called, began sailing across the relatively short stretch of the Caribbean to Florida. Many were caught doing so and sent back to Cuba by the United States. Others died trying.

In 1965, the United States and Cuba formalized an agreement that allowed America to airlift immigrants into the country. The airlift program lasted until 1994, when President Clinton stopped it because of changes in the makeup of the immigrants who were entering the United States. In the early years of the program, most of the immigrants were well educated and were quickly granted asylum. They were seen as being useful to

Miami has many Cuban immigrants.

American society. In the later years, the immigrants were mostly poor, uneducated people seeking to escape poverty. *Asylum* cannot be granted unless the immigrant risks persecution at home, and since poverty does not qualify as a "risk," the program was stopped.

Nearly two-thirds of all Cuban Americans live in Florida. The city of Miami has a district known as "Little Havana" (Havana is the capital of Cuba), which is primarily inhabited by Cuban immigrants. They faced many of the same problems that Mexican Americans did, but have been able to *integrate* into society somewhat more easily. Cuban Americans own and operate some of the most successful businesses in Florida, and the education levels of their children are at the national average.

Immigrants from the Dominican Republic

The Dominican Republic is a relatively new source of large numbers of immigrants. Approximately 400,000 Dominicans entered the United States between 1961 and 1986. The USCIS expects more than 700,000 Dominicans to be living in New York City during the early years of the twenty-first century, making them the fastest-growing minority group in the city. Dominicans are now the second largest Latino group in the northeastern United States.

Early Dominican immigrants were often mistaken for African American citizens because their skin is much darker than most other Latino peoples.

Dominican immigrants first began entering the United States around 1965, when they began fleeing repression at home. The Dominican army prevented Juan Bosch, the country's first democratically elected president, from taking office, leading to an uprising of outraged citizens supporting political change. The United States sent thousands of troops to the Dominican Republic to stop the violence. The U.S. troops sided with the Dominican army and stopped the revolt. An election plagued with violence and corruption followed, and an aide of the former dictator was elected president. The U.S. government realized that thousands of Dominican revolutionaries would likely be killed or jailed for the uprising and extended an offer to bring them to American soil. Ironically, for the next thirty years, Dominicans came to the United States seeking to escape the violence and corruption that the U.S. government had helped to foster.

43

drug cartels: a group
of businesses organized
to traffic illegal drugs.

oppressive: imposing a
harsh or cruel form of
dominance over some-
one.

South American Immigrants

ne of the major immigrant groups of South America comes from Colombia. The immigration from Colombia began in the 1960s with the arrival of more than 72,000 people. Early on, Colombian immigrants were typically well educated and willing to work. They were sought-after employees in the United States. As time passed, however, the political climate of Colombia changed, as did the type of people emigrating. Violence became more and more common throughout the country. *Drug cartels* grew in power. In 1997 alone, 31,000 people were killed. Colombians seeking to escape this violence and unrest fled the country rapidly.

Despite the violence and political unrest, Colombians do not usually qualify for political asylum. The United States and Colombia are partners in the global war on drugs, making it difficult for the United States to declare Colombia under the control of an *oppressive* government. The people in power in the United States do not want to lose this ally in their drug war by offending the Colombian government.

Many South Americans come to the United States for political reasons.

Central American Immigrants

n the late twentieth century, Central Americans seeking a better life began to immigrate in greater numbers to the

United States. During the 1970s, the immigration of people from countries like Nicaragua and El Salvador grew in response to the ongoing wars in those countries. Large numbers of children came in this wave of immigrants, fleeing after their parents had died in the fighting. Many American citizens felt these immigrants should be granted asylum, but the government declared they were fleeing for economic rather than political reasons and refused. Detention camps were established, and many were sent back to their home countries.

The Big Picture

t present, nearly one-third of all legal immigrants into the United States come from Latin American countries. Many still see the United States as the land of opportunity, and most are willing to work hard to achieve their dreams. The high rate of immigration, when combined with a large number of births in recent years, has made Latinos the largest minority group in the country.

Some non-Latinos fear that this will cause problems in the country. They claim that Latinos refuse to adopt "American" culture and customs. Discrimination against Latinos in the United States has ebbed and flowed throughout the country's history. Circumstances like the Great Depression have caused increases in prejudice that after a time tend to soften somewhat. One of the more recent upswings happened following the passage of laws in the 1990s that allowed employers to be fined if they hired illegal immigrants. Large portions of the public believed that illegal immigrants were all Latinos. As a result, employers began to ask for extensive documentation from all Latinos, even those who were American citizens. Although discrimination on the basis of national origin has been illegal in the United States for many years, employers began refusing to hire Latinos, even when prospective employees could present documentation, for fear of hiring someone with forged papers.

Today, some Americans who fear and dislike Latinos believe that Spanish-speaking

Immigrants from Central America bring with them the color and richness of their culture.

immigrants may never be absorbed fully into American society. Of course, other people point out that American culture and customs are nothing more than a hodgepodge of culture and customs from its many immigrants; how can something that is by its very nature taken from immigrants be harmed by immigrants? Immigrant groups form the foundation of American culture and customs. The influence of Latinos will certainly modify the culture and customs—but why should this make Americans nervous? It has already happened with countless other ethnic groups throughout America's history.

Habla Español

empleo (aim-play-oh): job

ley (lay): law

ciudad (see-oo-dahd): city

grupo (groo-poh): group

niño (neen-yoh): little boy

Getting in Legally: Nonimmigrant Visas

One of the adults, Ana, bustled over to where Concha sat with all the little ones. Ana scolded the children, "Don't bother the guest of honor. She has lived many years and deserves a chance to rest."

Concha smiled and reached for the baby in Ana's arms. "Ana, I love my niños. I don't mind talking with them. It is important for them to understand where they come from and why they are here. Why don't you tell them how you came to be here?"

A stamped passport

Ana sighed and perched on a nearby chair. She said quietly, "I don't know if I will be here that much longer. I came here to study at the university, to learn to be a doctor. I always thought I'd go back to Mexico to help my people, but now I don't know. That little baby deserves my help too. I just don't know what is best for her."

When Ana came into the United States, she was only intending to be here temporarily. As a result, the type of paperwork that she needed to come into the country was called a nonimmigrant visa. This general category of permits is for people who do not wish to have a permanent residence in the United States; these visas are not permanent. Each of the many individual categories of nonimmigrant visa has its own specific rules and guidelines. No one single visa covers all circumstances. The type of visa needed depends on what the applicant wants to do in the United States and how long she intends to stay. The nonimmigrant visa is a stamp in a traveler's passport that allows her to enter the United States for whatever purpose is stated on the visa application. Most often, potential travelers apply for visas at an American office in their home country, called an embassy or a consulate.

Nonimmigrant visas exist for many different categories. Categories of visas exist specifically for tourism and business, temporary workers, students, cultural exchange program participants, religious workers, journalists, fiancé visits, investors and financial planners, and airline or ship's crew members.

For the most part, visas allow a stay of more than six months but less than three years. Some types can be extended almost indefinitely, provided the holder applies for the extension before her visa runs out. In order to get an extension, the applicant must meet certain require-ments, which vary depending on the type of visa. Most visas are for an entire family, allowing a person to bring all immediate relatives along. This includes any children and a spouse. It does not mean, however, that a person can bring all of his relatives; the extended family must apply for their own visas if they wish to come along.

The most common types of visa granted each year are for students, temporary work-ers, tourists, and businesspeople. Business and tourist visas are by far the most common, as millions of people come to the country each year to visit or do business. Student visas, also known as F-1 visas, are granted to more than 500,000 individuals every year. They are the second most common type of visa used.

Business and Tourist Visa

he government acknowledges the need for a visa that allows individuals to travel to the country for business or pleasure. These people pump large quantities of money into the U.S. economy each year, and the government does not wish to discour-age them from doing so.

The B-1 visa is designed to allow travel into America for business. Individuals are only eligible for this visa if they are entering the country for business purposes. They cannot receive a salary of any kind from a U.S. business. In order to qualify for a B-1 visa, an indi-vidual must indicate that she is planning on doing business with a U.S. company in some way, and she must provide evidence to the U.S. government at one of their offices in the individual's home country. She must be able to explain her goals for the trip and give a list of activities planned while in the country. Another requirement is that she shows that she has sufficient money to complete the trip, either in personal savings or company sup-port. She must also prove that she has a permanent residence in her home country. The normal length of stay allowed on a B-1 visa is ninety days, with the possibility for an extension if proof can be provided that the stay must be longer.

A tourist, or B-2, visa allows individuals to enter the country for purposes other than work or study. It can be used for tourism, to receive medical treatment, to attend a funeral, to attend a wedding or other important celebration, or simply to visit relatives. In order to be eligible for this visa, individuals must show that they have maintained a permanent residence in their home country. It is also necessary to establish that the intent of the visit is to stay temporarily. Many government officials are suspicious that applicants for B-2 visas intend to stay and work in the United States, particularly if the individual is from a developing or *Third World* country. Being able to show evidence of a specific event that will be attended can help to convince the officer of the intent to visit and then return. The usual length of stay allowed by a B-2 visa is six months, with the possibility for an extension for another six months.

Citizens of some countries do not need to apply for a visa to visit the United States for business or pleasure. They are allowed to come and go with relative freedom, provided they do not stay more than ninety days. The U.S. Department of State puts countries on this list after it has been established that applicants from those countries almost always get visas when they apply.

Student Visa

hen students, like Ana in our story, want to study at an American university, school, or college, they apply for a student visa (F-1). If that school has been approved by the USCIS, they may be eligible to come to this country for that

If a child can learn English, he will be more apt to be accepted by colleges when he is older.

purpose. It is possible for a student to be accepted into the United States to attend a grade school or grammar school as well, though it is far less common for children than for young adults attending college. The individual must be accepted by the institution he is planning to attend and meet all requirements of that school, college, or university.

Most U.S. schools, colleges, and universities have English language requirements that must be met by all students. They use the Test of English as a Foreign Language (TOEFL) to determine the applicant's level of English. All that is really required to pass this exam is a basic knowledge of the language and the ability to communicate in English.

The individuals must show proof that they are going to be able to support themselves while in the United States. This can be through student loans, grants, and scholarships, as

A student in the United States with an F-1 visa
must return to her country when her education is complete.

well as family contributions. In addition, the applicants must prove that they are intending to return to their home country when they complete their program. No student is allowed to enter the United States using an F-1 if there is evidence that he may try to stay after he finishes school.

waiver: a document giving up a right or claim.

F-1 visa holders are allowed to work up to twenty hours per week while school is in session and full-time during breaks and vacations. The types of employment allowed are limited by USCIS regulations. Students may work any on-campus job, off-campus internship or co-op program, and residency or other practical training. In the event that an F-1 visa holder is struck by some bad luck and has severe financial difficulties, there is a process by which she can apply for a *waiver* of these rules. If accepted, she is allowed to work at any job of her choosing, but the rules for the number of hours per week do not change.

The spouses and children of F-1 visa holders are eligible for the F-2 visa, which allows the family to stay together. If a student is planning on bringing his family, he must prove that he has very strong financial support, because the family members are not allowed to work while in the country on the F-2 visa.

F-1 visa holders can stay for up to twelve months at the end of their schooling for additional training. Receiving practical training during the school career will cause the person to be ineligible for additional training. The additional training must be completed within fourteen months of completion of the school program.

Temporary Workers

he USCIS recognizes six categories of temporary worker visa, as defined by immigration law. Temporary workers have become very important to the U.S. economy because these individuals take positions that employers have trouble filling. Categories have been established for professional workers (H-1B), professional nurses (H-1C), temporary agricultural workers (H-2A), other temporary workers (H-2B), trainees (H-3), and the spouse or child of a person who qualifies for one of the other categories (H-4).

All temporary worker visas require that a nonimmigrant individual can only be hired to take a position for which the company cannot find a qualified U.S. citizen. The temporary visas are designed to allow companies to find workers in times of shortage by looking outside U.S. borders.

The most commonly assigned temporary worker visa is the H-1B. To qualify for H-1B status, an individual must have at least a four-year college degree or a combination of experience and education that is equivalent. If the job has a licensing requirement, the individual must hold the license before he enters the country. This program allows people who have been in the United States illegally to exit the country and then return as long as they apply for the visa outside the country. This rule separates this visa from many others.

Individuals cannot receive H-1B status by themselves. They must get an employer to submit a petition to the USCIS on their behalf indicating that they will have a job if the visa is granted. H1-B employers can be individuals, partnerships, or corporations. The USCIS requires that most employers pay a $1,000 training fee for all H-1B applicants they bring to work for them. The employer must pay the fee, and they cannot expect the individual to reimburse them for the payment. The company must also pay any attorney fees incurred by the applicant during the process of applying for the visa.

Employers must agree to pay the visa applicant the prevailing wage for the position they will be filling. This means the company has to pay the H-1B visa holder the same (or higher) wage rate as others in the country or the company doing the same sort of work. The company also has to pay the worker any benefits that others in the company enjoy. This requirement is designed to prevent employers from taking advantage of foreign workers.

An H-1B visa typically lasts for a three-year period, with the possibility for one three-year extension. Occasionally a person will be granted one additional extension, but this is rare. The visa can be taken away if general visa rules are broken.

Some workers qualify for TN status under the rules of the North American Free Trade Agreement (NAFTA), which allows them to apply for as many extensions as they wish. Only certain types of professionals can qualify for TN status, and NAFTA rules only apply to Mexican or Canadian citizens.

Foreign licensed practical or registered nurses who are willing to work in shortage areas can apply for an H1-C visa. Nonimmigrant nurses can now only be employed by U.S. hospitals and doctors' offices in areas that meet the USCIS guidelines for area of shortage. These visas are valid for up to three years. A nurse with a bachelor's degree can apply for and receive an H1-B visa instead of an H1-C if he meets the other requirements.

Temporary agricultural workers are a common sight on farms throughout the country. They enter America each year for harvest season and return to their home country when the crops are gone. This visa category was inspired by the Bracero Program that brought thousands of Mexican workers into the United States to work on farms. The difference between the Bracero Program and an H2-A visa is that the visa grants very specific rights and protections to the workers. Braceros were often severely underpaid and overworked. H2-A visa holders must be paid the prevailing wage in the same fashion as H1-B workers. The USCIS rules for H2-A visas require that there must be no qualified U.S. citizen available to take the job, and that the applicant will have a job when he reaches the country. This type of visa does not allow for extended stays, and often expires at the end of the harvesting period.

H2-B visas are reserved for those who might be useful to the U.S. workforce as temporary workers for new businesses or start-up projects. The positions cannot be long term. This visa typically expires within one year, and extensions are very rare. If an extension is

NAFTA

he North American Free Trade Agreement
(NAFTA) went into effect on January 1, 1994. NAFTA is
an attempt to establish a tariff-free trade area and to
remove barriers to investment between the United States,
Canada, and Mexico. There are provisions to add more
members. Proponents of NAFTA claim that its creation
will lead to more high-wage jobs in the United States and
an equalization between the economies of the member
countries. Not everyone sees it that way. Some U.S. critics
claim that the lifting of investment and trade restrictions
will send businesses (and their jobs) to the other members,
primarily to Mexico. Because the wages are so low there,
the business owners would see increasing profit margins
while the employees would be without a job. As can be
expected, many business owners are in favor of the agreement while many labor unions are not. Human rights
activists are also concerned about the effects of NAFTA,
since big businesses may exploit workers in countries where
there are fewer laws to protect workers and the environ-

ment. Businesses may find it cheaper to do business in countries like Mexico because they can get away with business practices American laws would never tolerate. Factories are often unsafe; dumping waste products into the environment is legal; workdays can be extremely long; and child labor is common. As the world's economy becomes more and more global, many people feel we also need global laws to protect the world's workers from unscrupulous corporations.

granted, the visas are limited to three years. It can be very difficult to get an H2-B visa because the types of work that qualify are often sought after by U.S. citizens.

Individuals who enter the United States on training assignments are eligible for the H-3 visa. In order to qualify, the specific training cannot be available in the person's home country. This visa allows the holder to work while training. The details of the training program must be given to the USCIS agent checking the application. H-3 visas are limited to two years.

Temporary workers who enter America are not all single and child-free. The H-4 visa was established for the families of temporary worker visa holders. The spouse and all dependents of any H visa holder can enter the United States on this visa. They are not allowed to work, but they can attend school or a training program while in the country.

Latino immigrants bring many assets to the United States.

In 2000, nearly 34 million nonimmigrant visas were granted by U.S. officials worldwide. The number dropped by more than 6 million in 2002, partly due to the attacks that occurred in the United States on September 11, 2001.

According to some estimates, the United States will suffer a shortage of 20 million workers by 2026. Alan Greenspan, the U.S. Federal Reserve Chairman, has said that shortages of this size could increase inflation and decrease the quality of life across the country.

Habla Español

visados (vee-sah-dohs): visas

comercio (coe-mare-see-oh): business

turista (too-rees-tah): tourist

estudiante (ace-too-dee-on-tay): student

Staying in Legally:
The Green Card

Concha looked around and saw the sad face of García. She said, "Why the long face, niño?"

"I am thinking of my brother in Mexico. He would not come when we came. He was too tough and independent. Now he wants to come, but he can't. My mama says that it will be years before he can join us."

Carmen asked García, "Why can't he just come?"

"Mamá says that he needs a colored card, but I don't know what that means."

Immigrants being sworn in as American citizens

Concha smiled. "I think you mean 'green card,' García."

"That's right! Green card. Mamá filled out a bunch of papers to get one for him, but they tell her it will be years before he can come. I don't understand why it takes so long. I miss *mi hermano!*"

Concha called the boy to her and gave him a hug. She said, "Miguel will be here eventually. For now, you just have to work hard in school and be a comfort to your mamá. She misses him too, you know."

Permanent Residents

The green card may be one of the most recognized pieces of plastic and paper in the entire world. The actual name of this card is the "Alien Registration Receipt Card." However, the term "alien" is offensive to many immigrants, and the real name is rarely used. The cards got their name from their color during the early years. Ironically, however, today's green cards are actually not green. The card issued now is pink. These cards have gone through many different colors over the years, including green, red, white, blue, and then finally, pink.

Many people mistakenly believe that green cards are nothing more than work permits for immigrants. Holding a green card does give an immigrant the right to work anywhere in the United States—but the green card's main function is to identify the holder as a permanent resident of the United States. This does not mean that he cannot leave and re-enter the country, just that he keeps a permanent residence within the country even when he leaves. In fact, one of the benefits of holding a greed card is the freedom to travel outside the United States, with the assurance of acceptance back into the country after the journey. Of course, the law places some limits on this; for instance, the holder must not stay away more than a year, or he risks losing his status.

Currently, although green cards give status as a "permanent" resident, the cards do expire ten years from the date they are received. The holder must replace the physical card every ten years or return to her home country. Fortunately, a simple renewal application is typically all it takes for a holder to get a new card, so long as she has a job and a residence.

Some people can get green cards more easily than others, depending on circumstances. Green card applicants fall into several different categories. Some types of cards are available immediately, while others are given based on a quota system, which means that only a certain number of that type are given each year. This type of system forces some people to wait many, many years for a green card of the type they need.

Different Types of Green Cards

he first and most desirable category of green cards is only for immediate relatives of U.S. citizens. Luckily for people with family who have already gone through the naturalization process or who were born in the United States, the USCIS has not set a quota for the number of this type of green card that can be issued. As a result, the USCIS has very strictly defined who qualifies as an immediate relative: the spouses of U.S. citizens, the unmarried children under age twenty-one of a U.S. citizen, parents of adult U.S. citizens, stepparents and stepchildren of U.S. citizens (so long as the marriage happened before the child turned eighteen), and adoptive parents and adoptive children of U.S citizens (if the adoption happened before the child turned sixteen).

Most other types of green cards are subject to a quota system, which limits the number issued in any given year. These green cards are given out using a preference system

A sign in Mexico points toward the U.S. border.

based on the applicant's country of origin and either family relationships or job skills. Family preference green cards were created to allow families to be reunited more quickly, even if they do not meet the immediate relative standards described above. People who are trying to get green cards based on their family relationships are divided into four categories, family first preference through family fourth preference. The family first preference category includes unmarried adults who have a parent who is a U.S. citizen. (Children under age twenty-one are immediate relatives and not subject to this system.) The family second preference is for spouses and unmarried children of green card holders. The married children of a U.S. citizen fall into the family third preference. Sisters and brothers of adult U.S citizens make up the family fourth preference. In order to get the green cards in this category, the person already in the United States must petition the USCIS for a green card for his family member.

The other category in the preference system is the employment preference-based group, which is divided into five subsets. These groupings are designed to allow easier access to green cards for people with job skills the government has decided are more desirable. The first preference is for outstanding people in art, science, education, business, or athletics, including managers and executives of multinational companies. Professionals with an advanced degree or outstanding ability make up the second preference. The employment third preference is for professionals or skilled and unskilled workers. Religious workers and various other types of workers are in the fourth preference. The fifth category is reserved for individuals willing to invest very large sums of money ($500,000 to $1 million, depending on where it is being invested) in an American business.

Congress determines how many visas in each of the preference categories described above will be available each year. Each

A Latino woman works as a seamstress in the 1950s.

preference is broken down further based on the country from which the applicants come, with different numbers being issued for immigrants from different countries. So, the length of time an immigrant will have to wait for her green card is determined by her country of origin and her preference category. Mexicans, for example, tend to wait much longer than people from all other countries except the Philippines. This wait happens because many people from Mexico would like green cards, and the government does not choose to give out nearly enough to meet the demand.

Unfortunately for people petitioning for green cards, the waiting lists can be exceptionally long. For example, a Mexican whose brother was a U.S. citizen and petitioned for him to get a green card in January 1992 did not get to move on in the application process until June 2004, more than twelve years later. The shortest waits in June 2004 for family-based green cards were still nearly four years. Mexicans had to wait at least seven years for a family-based green card. The wait tends to be much longer for family-based green cards than for employment-based green cards, which almost certainly reflects the U.S. government's preference for the middle- and upper-class immigrants who usually get these green cards.

The U.S. State Department issues a Visa Bulletin every month that shows which people are eligible to move on in the application process for a green card. This bulletin includes charts broken down by preference category and country of origin. The charts show dates, which represent when the original petition for a green card must have been filed. People who are waiting to apply must watch these bulletins to figure out, based on when they petitioned, when they can apply for a green card.

In addition, some green cards are given to immigrants from countries that have sent few immigrants in recent years. A block of green cards is set aside for people from these countries. These so-called Diversity Visas make sure the immigrant pool is varied. A computer randomly

Latino electronic workers

chooses the specific people who get these green cards; this process is referred to as the "green card lottery." No more than 55,000 of these were slated to be given out during 2004.

Workers who seek a first, second, or third preference employment-based green card must first obtain a labor certification from the U.S. Department of Labor. The process begins when a U.S. employer agrees to hire a foreign worker and petitions the department to get a certification that there are not enough qualified workers in the geographic area in question and that employing the foreign worker will not have a negative effect on the U.S. labor market. Unfortunately, the department takes approximately one year to process the certifications. In order to get one, the employer must prove four things:

A Latino man works as a chef.

1. The job offered to the foreign worker is open to people in the United States.
2. The job has no unreasonable or unnecessary conditions placed on it.
3. The foreign worker will be paid at least the prevailing wage in the community.
4. The employer made reasonable efforts to fill the position with U.S. citizens or permanent residents.

The Department of Labor has set the minimum qualifications for most jobs. Even if the foreign worker is more qualified than the U.S. workers who apply for the position, the employer cannot hire the foreign worker unless no U.S. workers apply who meet the department's minimum qualification. What this means in practicality is that there are no green cards for unskilled workers, because there is almost always someone in the United States who can meet the minimum qualifications. An employer must be very serious about hiring the foreign worker, because the delay and the administrative burden of the application process will scare away many employers. The U.S. government almost certainly chose to make the process difficult in an effort not to flood the U.S. labor market with foreign workers.

Individuals who are seeking green cards based on family relationships, whether they are immediate relatives or relations who fall within the family-based preference categories, are treated by the law as if they are likely to become a public charge. This presumption also applies if the employer who seeks an employment-based green card is a relative of the potential foreign worker. Whatever is written at the base of the Statue of Liberty about bringing in the poor, tired, huddled masses, modern immigration policy does not encourage people to come to America without the financial means to support themselves!

To that end, in order to get a green card based on family relationships, each immigrant must have a sponsor who will swear that he is willing and able to support the immigrant. The sponsor has to make enough money to support himself, his family, and the new immigrant. The new immigrant cannot collect welfare or many other needs-based government programs until she has been in the country for five years. Even after she has been here for five years, she will only be eligible for those programs if her sponsor has fallen on extremely hard times.

Some green cards are issued each year under special laws that designate them for specific groups, allowing people in these groups, called special immigrants, to avoid the preference system. These groups include certain religious workers, doctors who have been in the United States since 1978, foreign workers who were longtime employees of the U.S. government, and several other special groups.

The USCIS recognizes the need for America to accept refugees and asylees from other countries. In order to fall under one of these categories, people must file paperwork showing that they fear political or religious persecution in their home country. The difference between refugees and asylees is that refugees ask permission before entering the United States, and asylees wait until they are already in the country before filing. The President of the United States sets the number of refugees who will be accepted into the country each year from certain regions of the world. Refugees and asylees can apply for green cards after they have been in the country legally for one year. Refugees are subject to the President's quota before entering and are therefore not subject to a quota when seeking a green card. Asylees, on the other hand, are not subject to any quota before becoming asylees and are therefore subject to one before getting a green card.

An individual who successfully completes the green card application process will be issued an immigrant visa, which allows him to legally enter the United States if he is not already there within the six months after it is issued. Once the immigrant visa is issued, he can claim his green card.

Green card holders must meet two basic requirements in order to keep their card for life. First, they must maintain their permanent residence in the United States for life. Second, they must not commit a removable offense, such as a violent crime or possession of drugs.

This Mexican man lived most of his life in the United States—but was deported for committing a misdemeanor.

Most visas, including the immigrant visas people need to claim their green cards, are issued in foreign countries at the U.S. offices in those countries. However, the law acknowledges that many applicants for green cards will already be inside the United States and has created a process called Adjustment of Status. This process allows an individual who is in the country on a nonimmigrant visa (for example, a student or a temporary worker) to apply to change their status from nonimmigrant to immigrant, meaning that they intend to stay in the country. Unfortunately for many individuals, the law does not allow people who have overstayed their visas or failed to follow other rules, making them "out of status," to benefit from this process.

Habla Español

mi hermano (mee air-mon-oh): my brother

tarjetas verde (tahr-hay-tahs vare-day): green cards

familia (fah-mee-lee-ah): family

STEWART

The Law and Citizenship

"Grandma, cheer us up! Please tell us a happy story," cried Carmen, trying to distract everyone from sad thoughts.

Concha sat back in her chair and asked, "Do you want to hear about the day I got married or the day I became a citizen? Those are two of my happiest days."

The little ones debated it among themselves for a moment, but Carmen decided on the second option.

Concha cleared her throat and started her story. "I was no longer a young woman. I had been here for many years by that time, and I was married and had three grown children. They were all citizens already, because they were born in this country. Luis, my youngest son, was the first one in the family to go to college. Carmen, that is your grandfather I am talking about. He came home after his first year with the idea that I needed to become a citizen. Although I had discovered that America was not the magic place I thought it was when I was a young child, I have loved my adopted country since we arrived. I agreed to make it my own.

"It wasn't easy. I knew I would have to pass a test on the history and government of this country. I never went to school here, and I only knew what I had picked up helping the kids study for history tests and reading the newspaper over the years. Luis helped me study, and I learned. I learned about the Constitution and this country's presidents and much, much more.

"I had to fill out papers, and eventually I had to take the test. I passed! I was so happy. The whole family came to watch me take my oath of allegiance to this country. It was a very happy day!"

Winning the Prize

he top prize for most immigrants is citizenship and all that comes with it. Becoming a U.S. citizen is sometimes considered the "holy grail" of immigration law, because citizenship offers benefits and protections that visas and green cards do not. United States immigration law lays out many rules that must be met for a noncitizen to enter the country.

It has been said that some parts of immigration law were actually designed to stop immigration because they are so complex. Most often, a lawyer is needed to interpret the wording of the laws, making immigration expensive and time-consuming.

Citizenship is something that most Americans take for granted every day. Once we

New American citizens

Democracy is a benefit of citizenship.

turn eighteen, we can vote for elected officials, though many people rarely, if ever, take advantage of that benefit. Though voting may not always seem like such a benefit, consider that in some countries the people are ruled by someone who answers to no one. In the United States, elected officials who continually ignore the people do not tend to have long careers.

Participation in democracy is one of the most powerful benefits of citizenship, but it is not the only one. United States citizens can leave the country for extended periods and not worry about being able to return. They may carry U.S. passports to prove their citizenship. Visas and green cards expire; citizenship does not. A citizen can live anywhere in the world for as long as she wants and return at any time as a full citizen. In addition, individuals with a green card or visa may find themselves deported if they commit a crime; not so for citizens. Citizens pass on their citizenship to their children, even if they are born in another country. Citizens can sponsor relatives for green cards, whereas noncitizens have only very limited rights to do so.

According to the U.S. Constitution, all people born in the country (except the children of foreign *diplomats*) are granted automatic citizenship. The process of becoming a U.S. citizen is called naturalization. Most of the time, in order to become a naturalized citizen, an individual must first apply for and receive a green card. To qualify for naturalization, an individual must have been a green card holder in the United States for a minimum period of time. For most people, the amount of time required is five years. An immigrant hoping to apply for citizenship must maintain a permanent residence in this country for the entire five-year period. In addition, an individual seeking citizenship and holding a green card may be physically outside the country for no more than one-half of that five-year period.

Latina women working in food preparation

Leaving the country without returning for more than one year causes the time period to restart. In other words, if Concha had already held her green card for a number of years and then left the country for more than one year, she would have to start the time period over and she would not have been able to naturalize for five more years. In addition, such an absence would have put her at risk of losing her green card. If she had gone out of the country for more than six months but less than one year, she would have reset the waiting period unless she could show proof of having kept a home in the United States, such as pay stubs or rent receipts.

Some factors can reduce the amount of time it takes to become a citizen. Being married to a U.S. citizen shortens the amount of time a person needs to wait while holding a green card to three years. Refugees and people who came seeking asylum in the United States have to hold their green cards for only four years. However, all of the other rules still apply.

In order to qualify for citizenship through naturalization, Concha would have had to meet other requirements. She would have had to have lived at least three months in the area in which she filed her application. She would also have had to show that she had "good moral character" and that she had maintained it for the five years prior to applying for citizenship. Some examples of the sorts of things that damage moral character enough to prevent naturalization include theft, murder or other violent *felonies*, possession of drugs, any jail term of more than 180 days, and putting false information in any immigration paperwork. The USCIS agent in charge of the application decides what constitutes poor moral character, but these are some of the things that tend to influence those decisions. In addition, *community service* or other noble activities can positively influence the decision.

Applying for Citizenship

The actual application process is fairly straightforward. Concha would have filled out the paperwork and filed it at the local USCIS office (though it would have been called by a different name when she applied for citizenship). An agent processed the application, which can take up to a year in some parts of the country. Then Concha would have gone in for an interview, or an oral test, that must be passed to become a citizen. Agents would have asked her many questions about U.S. history and government. Of course, many people born in this country would have trouble answering these questions, in spite of having sat through high school history, but Concha would have had to become familiar with the material before she could become a citizen. She would have had to demonstrate that she could read, write, and speak English as well. Older applicants who have been in the country for many years have less strict requirements, and persons with disabilities can get special accommodations.

Sometimes the USCIS will reject an application for naturalization. The rejection always includes a list of reasons for the decision and all paperwork and instructions for fil-

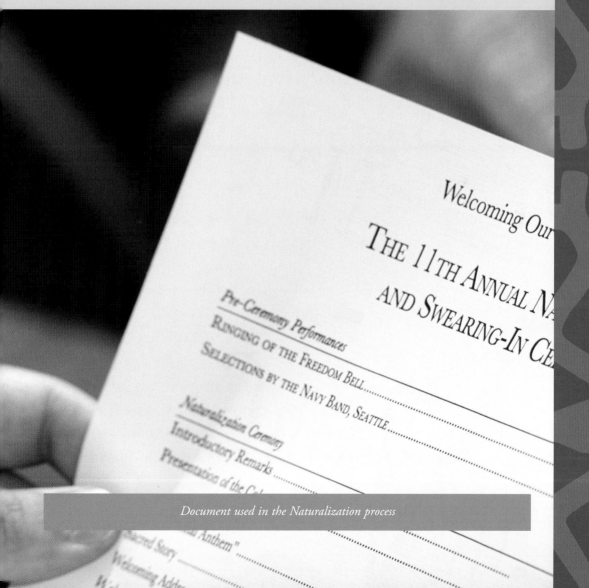

Document used in the Naturalization process

New Americans

ing an administrative *appeal*. The rejected applicant has the right to a hearing with the USCIS to review the application and the reasons for the refusal. If the applicant is not successful at the hearing, he can appeal through the court system. However, a court appeal is very complicated and is far more likely to be successful with the assistance of an experienced immigration lawyer. Another strategy following a rejection is to correct the problems mentioned in the original rejection and then reapply. Of course, anyone with a serious flaw in his application, especially relating to moral character, is at risk of having his green card taken away if he calls too much attention to himself.

A Citizen at Last

he final step in the naturalization process is the swearing-in ceremony, where an applicant takes an oath of allegiance to the United States and swears to follow the Constitution. At the completion of the swearing-in ceremony, the applicant and any of her children under eighteen who also hold green cards become U.S. citizens. Many new citizens, like Concha, treat the long-awaited event as a cause for great celebration.

The new citizen gains the right to vote and all other rights of U.S. citizens. Once she becomes a citizen, she will always be a citizen, no matter what. She can travel freely, live abroad, even be convicted of crimes, without fear of losing her citizenship.

he process of becoming a citizen is somewhat easier for older people who have been in the country for extended periods of time. Applicants between the ages of fifty and fifty-five who have been in the country for twenty years do not have to read, write, and speak English. If they are over fifty-five and have been here fifteen years, they are also exempt. Applicants over sixty-five who have been in the country more than twenty years can take a much shorter oral test, with 90 percent fewer questions than during a normal interview.

Habla Español

cuidadano (kwee-dah-dah-no): citizen

jurar la bandera (hoo-rahr la bon-day-rah): becoming a citizen; literally means "to swear to the flag"

Through the Back Door: Illegal Immigration

The little ones continued to chatter while Concha looked around the room to make sure everyone was still enjoying themselves. She may have been the guest of honor at this party, but she was still a hostess at heart. Concha's grandson, Jorge, was flirting with some of the attractive neighbor girls on the other side of the room. When he saw her watching him, he smiled and excused himself immediately. He weaved in and out of the crowd, exchanging pleasantries in Spanish on his way over. When he arrived, he bent to kiss her cheek and wished her a happy birthday.

Mexicans with the proper papers walk across the bridge to the United States.

The children's attention returned to Concha and the newcomer. Jorge had not been in the country very long, and many of the children did not know him well.

Carmen, bold as usual, said, "Jorge, we've been hearing stories all afternoon. Why don't you tell us yours?"

Jorge smiled and responded, "Okay, young cousin, what would you like to hear?"

Carmen had overheard some of the older people talking about Jorge, and she knew he had had some sort of adventure on his way into the country. "Tell us how you came to America!"

Jorge smiled. "I will just tell you the short story, because I need to get back to my friends. Several months ago, I decided the time had come to visit El Norte. Much of my family was here, and there wasn't much to hold me in Mexico anymore. I took a bus from my home to northern Mexico, where I had heard I could find a man to help me get across the border into Arizona. I found the man I was looking for, a young hombre with a baseball hat and much gold jewelry.

"I paid him 750 U.S. dollars for his help. Many of us, mostly all young men, were driven in a van out into the desert. We carried a couple bottles of water and a few other things in our bags. We started walking. We walked and walked, following a man who said he knew where we were going. We walked all day and into the night. I finished my water, and I was very thirsty and weak. The man told us that we were crossing into America now, and we would be safe soon. Just when we started to believe we would make it, we heard the noise of a helicopter. Soon, we were flooded with light from above. The helicopter landed, and we were surrounded by men in uniforms, all speaking English very quickly. They gave us some water, and after an hour or two, they loaded us onto a bus that had come to take us away. It was horrible. They took us right back to Mexico and dropped us across the border.

"I don't give up easily, though. After a few days of rest, I tried again. This time I made it, and here I am!"

Marker indicating the border between the U.S. and Mexico

A Rising Tide

he USCIS estimated that there were about 7 million illegal immigrants in the United States in the early part of 2000. This number was estimated to be growing by about 500,000 each year, a figure arrived at by calculating the number of new illegal immigrants entering the country minus the number leaving, becoming legal, or dying each year. If the numbers are even close to the truth, between 8 million and 9 million illegal immigrants live and work in the country. Some organizations estimate the numbers to be much higher, closer to 15 million.

The focus of the USCIS in the past few years has been to discover the factors that influence illegal immigration. In order to control the inflow of illegal immigrants, they must understand what brings them here. Surveys conducted of illegal immigrants being removed from the country indicate that the two most common reasons for entering the country were family ties and work.

Communities with high concentrations of Latino families exist throughout the United States. Immigrants usually find it easier to locate work and homes in areas where other immigrants live, in part because they have the support of other families who have lived through the stress of immigrating to America. Latino families tend to be very close, and the communities usually reflect the respect for family and elders shared by most Latinos.

In much of the United States, Latino illegal immigrants who are desperate to support their families take the lowest-paying jobs. They will work long hours for a wage that is barely sufficient to pay the bills because there is even less opportunity for them in their home country. A Mexican immigrant, for example, might take a job that pays minimum wage (or less, though it is illegal) in a factory and move his whole family to the United States. He cannot make this wage in Mexico, where many jobs do not pay well enough for people to support their families. They come across the border seeking better pay, not knowing or not caring that the wage they will receive is far below what is considered the poverty level for this country.

Legal Latino immigrants are often involved in helping illegal immigrants enter and stay in the United States. Typically, they help get family members across the border to reunite their families. Latino business owners are sometimes willing to risk fines or deportation to help others. They will give illegal immigrants jobs, which is in violation of immigration law. They can lose their livelihood for doing this, but the family ties are important enough for them to risk it.

Illegal immigrants to the United States must often cross hot, barren land.

89

humanitarian: committed to improving the lives of others.

The Border Patrol

he U.S. Border Patrol is charged with controlling the flow of illegal immigrants into the country. In areas all along the U.S.-Mexico border, patrol units attempt to maintain control. In some areas, their job is made easier by fences, walls, and checkpoints. In other areas, especially desert or mountainous areas, nothing marks the border at all. The border is patrolled by armed men in cars and helicopters and by high-tech equipment with motion-sensing and heat-sensing cameras.

The Border Patrol's job is made far more difficult by the work of individuals who specialize in avoiding the Border Patrol and smuggling people into the country illegally for money. *Coyote* is the name given to these people. Hopeful individuals and families flock to towns near the border, willing to risk their lives for a chance to enter the United States. They are willing to pay all the money they have for one attempt. The coyotes will collect groups of people to maximize their profits before making the crossing. At times, hundreds of people wait in these towns for their chance to cross. The coyotes offer no guarantees of success or even survival. Most people believe they do what they do for money, not because they care about the people they are "helping." Of course, networks of individuals assisting with illegal immigration for *humanitarian* reasons do exist all across the Southwest and on both sides of the border.

The crossing can be deadly. Each year, many people die trying to sneak past the Border Patrol when they agree to let the

Border Patrol returns an illegal entrant in handcuffs.

The long fence between Mexico and the United States

coyotes seal them into boxcars of northbound trains or pack them into refrigerated trucks. The grisly finding of dozens of dead people in railcars has alerted the Border Patrol to this strategy. In the past, border crossings were done near urban centers, where illegal immigrants could move about the cities without much risk of being caught, but the efforts of the Border Patrol have changed that. Advancements in technology have allowed them to control these areas much more effectively, so the coyotes don't operate there as much as they once did. In fact, border crossings now tend to happen in places far from any towns or cities. The conditions along these regions of the border are dangerous for many trying to enter the United States illegally. Elderly individuals cannot be expected to make the twenty-five-mile walk from the border to the nearest town in Arizona, but they try. The coyotes who often facilitate these crossings often take people who are ill-equipped for the journey, either because of weakness or lack of supplies and water, resulting in more deaths.

It has been said that the U.S.-Mexico border is "like a long, skinny balloon." The Border Patrol squeezes one area, stopping illegal immigration in that place, but other parts of the balloon bulge out. Every time the patrol finds a way to stop a leak in one area, a leak in another area springs up. The border is just too long to easily control. Too many people are desperate to enter the country, and the law permits too few of them to enter legally. Anyone willing to keep trying will eventually find a way past the Border Patrol—or die trying.

Habla Español

frontera (frone-tare-ah): border

primo (pree-moe): cousin

Mañana

The party was winding down, and Concha was tired. She had loved having her family and friends around her, but she was ready to go home. Over the last few minutes, a steady stream of people who were getting ready to leave had come to hug and kiss her goodbye. She had managed to pull herself out of the comfortable chair she'd been sitting in for the last couple of hours and take her leave of all the children.

The crowded border crossing

After saying her last goodbyes, Concha started out the door. Her daughter had offered to drop her at home and save her having to take the bus. Just as she was leaving, she felt the same small tug on her skirt that she had felt earlier. She turned to see Carmen again, smiling up at her.

"Abuela, thank you for all your stories. Will you come tell some more again soon?"

"I am always glad to tell you stories, *niña*. Someday, though, you will be the one telling stories to your little people. Maybe then you will tell them about the way it used to be when our people couldn't freely come and go, when people had to wait years or sneak through the desert to come here. Mañana, little one!"

he United States has been the "land of opportunity" for immigrants for many decades. The people of America have become more and more aware of immigration issues every year. Stories make the news frequently about the deaths of dozens of people trying to enter the country illegally. September 11, 2001, also brought immigration to the forefront, since the perpetrators of the terrorist acts were all noncitizens. As a result, these issues have become part of the public's awareness of immigration over the past several years.

Latino factory workers

Feeling the pressure to change the immigration system, politicians constantly search for the answer to the problem of illegal immigration. In the past few years, the media have seen three hot topics tossed around as solutions to some of the ongoing problems with immigration policy for Latinos.

Guest Worker

uest worker programs are designed to allow immigrant workers to enter the United States to work on a temporary basis. Historically, these programs have been in response to a lack of workers within the country. The first of these, called the Bracero Program, was instituted in 1917 as a countermeasure to the lack of farm workers during World War I. During that time, there was no U.S. Border Patrol, and many of the braceros did not return to their home countries when the program ended in

Latino farmworker

1921. In addition to this, many of the farmers did not pay the workers a living wage for their work, which increased poverty throughout the country.

The second Bracero Program began in 1942. It was actually a series of agreements between the United States and Mexico that allowed approximately 4.6 million Mexicans to enter and work legally in the United States. Interestingly, the admission of Mexicans was lowest during World War II, when the country needed as many workers as it could get. The peak during the war came in 1944, when only about 62,000 individuals came across the border. The overall peak was during 1956, when farms brought in nearly 450,000 workers.

The U.S. and Mexican governments realized that the "temporary" admission of workers into the United States was not working the way it was intended. Many farmers became dependent on the inexpensive migrant workers, and the workers did not return to Mexico as planned. Landowners stopped trying to fill positions on their farms with more expensive local workers. They would employ the migrant workers year round, even though the Bracero Program agreement required workers to return to Mexico. The workers and their families became dependent on the income provided by the farmers. The braceros often signed contracts written in English, which they could not even read, and were forced to work for far less than they expected. They were paid wages that caused some citizens to compare the program to government-approved slavery. Faced with such problems, the program was ended in 1964. The Immigration Reform and Control Act of 1986 established for the first time the responsibility of the employer not to employ illegal immigrants in an effort to stop the use of braceros remaining in the country.

The end of the Bracero Program was not the end of the

For those living in slums along the U.S. border, America looks like a land of riches.

migrant worker. Recognizing that the need for temporary workers remained, a new category of visa was developed. The H visa is a nonimmigrant permit that allows a person to enter the United States to work for a limited time. This type of visa allows an individual to apply for permits that would allow him to remain in the United States for up to three years, with the possibility for an extension at the end. In order to qualify for this visa, an individual must have a U.S. business sponsor them. The employer is required to file paperwork on behalf of the applicant. This was designed to prevent the types of abuse that doomed the Bracero Program.

President George W. Bush has acknowledged that illegal immigration continues to be a major problem in the United States. On January 7, 2004, President Bush went before the public to announce a push for new immigration laws that would allow guest workers to enter and work in the United States on a temporary basis. It would attempt to match willing workers to unfilled job openings in the United States. Although many believed that the program was proposed in an attempt to gain Latino votes in the 2004 election, public sentiment toward the program seemed to be fairly negative. The people who traditionally dislike immigration obviously did not like the program. In addition, many Latino advocates did not believe the program went far enough, because it would eventually force participants to go back to their own country. As of the writing of this book, few details about the proposed program are known, and nothing has happened to move it toward actual passage.

Amnesty

resident Bush's proposed temporary worker program contains elements of what has been traditionally known as amnesty, which allows illegal immigrants to change their status from illegal to legal. President Bush has been careful to indicate that what he has proposed is *not* amnesty. However, the program would allow illegal immigrant workers to remain in the United States, provided they are applying for a green card and pay a $1,000 fine. It is designed to benefit those already in the country who may have entered illegally or overstayed their visas. Applicants for this particular amnesty offer must have been living and working in the United States prior to August 2001 and be able to show proof of employment or have been married to a U.S. citizen before that date. All applicants must be sponsored by their employer or spouse. Individuals who have had children born in America can be sponsored by their children, if the children are old enough to be considered citizens.

This would not be the first time an amnesty offer has been extended to illegal immigrants. Many politicians have, at different times, attempted to address the issue of illegal immigrants living and working in the United States. The most popular options have been

Waiting to enter America

to either round up and deport illegal immigrants or offer them amnesty in hopes they will come forward to apply for legal status. The U.S. Census Bureau estimates that there are approximately 8 to 11 million illegal immigrant workers in the country at this time, making the first option, deportation, very expensive and time-consuming.

Amnesty was offered to illegal immigrants when the Immigration Reform and Control Act of 1986 passed. The INS allowed certain individuals the opportunity to legalize their residence in the United States. Illegal immigrants who had been in the country four or more years could receive a green card without fear of being deported. More than 2.8 million illegal immigrants came forward during this amnesty period.

An amnesty program has two major benefits for the government. First, a number of illegal immigrants will come forward to apply because, while they do wish to obey the law, they wish to stay in the country more. Previous amnesty programs have always been met with a rush of applicants as illegal immigrants hoping they can be legal residents come forward. This will give the government a better count of how many illegal immigrants are in the country, which can be very important for national security and future immigration policy. Second, those that receive amnesty pay a $1,000 fine and become part of the government tax lists. They will no longer work "under the table" at the expense of working citizens.

Open Borders

he term *open borders* is used to describe a concept that some Latinos have talked about for many years. American borders today are far from open, though some immigrants would certainly like them to be. Under an open-borders policy, people would be allowed to come and go from the United States freely. Some people have proposed open borders within North America; others suggest opening them to South America or even the whole world.

Advocates believe an open-borders policy would be very good for tourism, allowing free movement of people back and forth with fewer problems. Open borders would allow people to cross the U.S.-Mexico border coming to work, vacation, and visit relatives in the United States. Supporters argue that such a policy could be very good for the economies of both countries.

Many people in the United States, however, have very negative views on this policy. In some sections of the country, Latinos outnumber Anglo-Europeans, and there is a good deal of anti-Latino sentiment among the minority. The feeling in some areas is that Latino immigrants are taking good jobs away from U.S. citizens and are a drain on social programs like welfare. These people see Latinos as a threat to the "American" way of life, and they view immigration, especially of Latinos, as a threat to our national identity.

Latinos, they argue, refuse to merge with other cultures, creating isolated barrios instead of living in mixed societies.

Other people argue that allowing open borders is the only way to go. They believe that free movement of workers and families across the borders would actually relieve the ill effects of illegal immigration. The jobs that illegal immigrants take are typically low-skill ones and do not pay all that well. Many of these jobs remain unfilled without immigrants to fill them; U.S. citizens are unlikely to take these jobs at all. The effect on social programs would also be limited, they say, because many of the immigrants are from Mexico, and they would return to their homes at the end of the workday.

uest worker programs, amnesty, and open borders are all ways to make the United States more accessible to Latino Americans. Feelings about these programs continue to be mixed, and, as of the writing of this book, none of them appear to be too close to becoming reality.

But regardless of official policies, many Latinos will continue to come to America. Life in the United States has much to offer—and these immigrants will offer much to America as well.

A long line waits to cross from Mexico into the United States.

Habla Español

mañana (mon-yon-ah): tomorrow

abierto (ah-bee-air-toe): open

Timeline

1845—United States annexes Texas.

1875—The U.S. Supreme Court rules that immigration is a federal, not a state, responsibility.

1882—Congress passes the first immigration law.

1891—Immigration Act of 1891 goes into effect, considered by many the first immigration policy.

1906—Congress passes the Basic Naturalization Act.

1917—U.S. Immigration Service is founded.

1924—National Origins Quota system begins as part of the Immigration Act of 1924.

1924—U.S. Border Patrol is established.

1933—Immigration and Naturalization Service (INS) is established.

1994—Operation Gatekeeper begins.

September 11, 2001—Terrorists attack New York City and Washington, D.C.

Further Reading

Acuña, Rodolfo F. *U.S. Latino Issues.* Westport, Conn.: Greenwood Press, 2003.

Andryszewski, Tricia. *Immigration: Newcomers and Their Impact on the United States.* Brookfield, Conn.: Millbrook Press, 1995.

Ashabranner, Brent, and Paul Conklin. *Our Beckoning Borders: Illegal Immigration to America.* New York: Cobblehill Books, 1996.

Barbour, Scott. *Immigration Policy.* San Diego, Calif.: Greenhaven Press, 1995.

Barnett, Tracy L. *Immigration from South America.* Philadelphia: Mason Crest, 2004.

Figueredo, D. H. *The Complete Idiot's Guide to Latino History and Culture.* Indianapolis, Ind.: Alpha Books, 2002.

Gay, Kathlyn. *Leaving Cuba: From Operation Pedro Pan to Elian.* Brookfield, Conn.: Twenty-First Century Books, 2000.

Gelletly, Leann, Stuart Anderson, and Peter A. Hammerschmidt. *Mexican Immigration.* Philadelphia: Mason Crest, 2004.

Gonzalez, Juan. *Harvest of Empire: A History of Latinos in America.* New York: Viking, 2000.

Hauser, Pierre. *Illegal Aliens.* Philadelphia: Chelsea House, 1997.

Hernandez, Roger E., Stuart Anderson, and Peter A. Hammerschmidt. *Cuban Immigration.* Philadelphia: Mason Crest, 2004.

Hernandez, Romel, Stuart Anderson, and Peter A. Hammerschmidt. *Immigration from Central America.* Philadelphia: Mason Crest, 2004.

Morrow, Robert. *Immigration: Blessing or Burden?* Minneapolis, Minn.: Lerner Publications, 1997.

Schell, Debbie M., Richard E. Schell, and Kurt A. Wagner. *U.S. Immigration and Citizenship Q & A.* Naperville, Ill.: Sphinx Publishing, 2003.

Sonneborn, Liz. *The Cuban-Americans.* San Diego, Calif.: Lucent Books, 2002.

For More Information

Ellis Island History
www.nps.gov/elis

Immigration History and Policy
immigration.about.com/cs/
immigranthistory/index_2.htm

Immigration Overview
memory.loc.gov/learn/features/immig/
immigration_set1.html

Information about Cuba
www.afrocubaweb.com

Information about El Salvador
www.ecst.csuchico.edu/~william

Information about Puerto Rico
www.centropr.org

Mexican American History
www.digitalhistory.uh.edu/mexican_
voices/mexican_voices.cfm

Overview of Immigration Policy
www.immihelp.com

PBS New Americans Series
www.pbs.org/kcet/newamericans

USCIS and Immigration History
uscis.gov/graphics/aboutus/history/index
.htm

U.S. Immigration Facts
www.rapidimmigration.com/usa/1_eng_
immigration_facts.html

U.S. Immigration Policy
www.closeup.org/immigrant.htm

Publisher's note:
The Web sites listed on this page were active at the time of publication. The publisher is not responsible for Web sites that have changed their addresses or discontinued operation since the date of publication. The publisher will review and update the Web site list upon each reprint.

Index

Picture Credits

Benjamin Stewart: pp. 31, 42, 66, 72, 86, 87, 91, 95, 99, 101, 105

Corel: pp. 44, 46

The Jesús Colón papers, Centro de Estudios Puertorriqueños, Hunter College, CUNY, photographer unknown: p. 25

The Justo A. Marti Photographic Collection, Centro de Estudios Puertorriqueños, Hunter College, CUNY, photographer unknown: p. 29

Library of Congress: p. 34

PhotoDisc: pp. 50, 54, 64, 75, 77, 78, 81, 82

Photos.com: pp. 10, 53, 60, 63, 85, 89, 92, 96, 102

The Records of the Offices of the Government of Puerto Rico in the U.S., Centro de Estudios Puertorriqueños, Hunter College, CUNY, photographer unknown: pp. 9, 11, 19, 22, 33, 37, 49, 67, 69, 70, 79, 97, 98

Biographies

Miranda Hunter lives near Buffalo, New York. She received a B.A. from Geneva College and a J.D. from the University at Buffalo School of Law. Miranda recently changed careers to become a high school teacher.

Dr. José E. Limón is professor of Mexican-American Studies at the University of Texas at Austin where he has taught for twenty-five years. He has authored over forty articles and three books on Latino cultural studies and history. He lectures widely to academic audiences, civic groups, and K–12 educators.